Uncle Jo's Old Coat

by

Eleanora H. Stooke

Double 9 BOOKS

Uncle Jo's Old Coat

by Eleanora H. Stooke

ISBN: 978-93-67143-79-7

Published by

DOUBLE 9 BOOKS

2/13-B, Ansari Road
Daryaganj, New Delhi – 110002
info@double9books.com
www.double9books.com
Tel. 011-40042856

ABOUT THE AUTHOR

Eleanora H. Stooke was an author best known for her contributions to children's literature. Her works often explore themes of family, memory, and the emotional connections we form with the world around us. Stooke's storytelling is characterized by its warmth and relatability, making her stories resonate with young readers and their families.

One of her most notable works is "Uncle Jo's Old Coat," which illustrates the significance of cherished belongings and the memories they hold. Through her engaging narratives, Stooke encourages readers to appreciate the bonds of love and the importance of preserving memories across generations. Stooke's ability to blend gentle life lessons with charming storytelling has left a lasting impact in the realm of children's literature, ensuring her stories continue to be enjoyed by new generations. While not as widely recognized as some of her contemporaries, her contributions remain valuable for their heartfelt exploration of childhood experiences and family ties.

CONTENTS

Chapter I
Unexpected News

"OH, Jo, such news! I don't know whether I'm pleased or not; but I do hope it will be for the best!" And so saying, the speaker, Mrs. Dennis, laid down the letter she had been reading and glanced at her husband, with a smile upon her lips and tears in her eyes.

It was half-past eight on a fine September morning, and the Dennis family—comprised of Dr. Dennis, his wife, and three children, Edwin and Claude, aged eleven and nine respectively, and Poppy, a bright little maiden of eight—were seated at the breakfast-table. Four pairs of eyes turned curiously upon Mrs. Dennis as she spoke, and her husband hastened to inquire:

"What is it, my dear? What is it you hope will be for the best? That is a letter from your brother, is it not?"

"Yes, in which he informs me that he is going to be married again; and he wants us to have Freddy to stay with us for a few months whilst he and his bride are away on their wedding trip. Here, Jo—" and as she spoke Mrs. Dennis handed the letter to her husband— "read what he says for yourself."

The children, who had been listening with great interest, exchanged glances of mingled surprise and excitement. Freddy was their cousin, a boy of nine years old, the only child of their mother's brother, Mr. Frederick Collins, a landowner in Devonshire, who lived at a beautiful old home called Marldon Court. Mr. Collins had been left a widower when his little son had been only a few months old, consequently Freddy had never known a mother's love; but he had never been conscious of anything wanting in his life, for his father had made him his first care, and the servants at Marldon Court had always humoured his slightest whim. Mrs. Dennis had been in the habit of spending a week or so with her brother every spring, taking one of her children with her; this year it had been Edwin's turn, and he had, therefore, the most vivid recollections of his cousin, and was not altogether charmed at the prospect of having him as a visitor in the house.

"I don't think Freddy would care to be here," he remarked soberly; "he's so fond of the country, and he'd find our home very poky and dull. I hope he won't come!"

"That sounds an inhospitable speech, considering the enjoyable fortnight you spent at Marldon Court not so long ago," his mother said, in a tone of gentle reproof. "Why should you wish your cousin not to come?"

Edwin flushed, and made no reply. He did not wish to appear inhospitable; but, as he mentally compared the handsome dining-room at Marldon Court with the decidedly shabby apartment in which they were breakfasting, he doubted if Freddy would be contented with the change from the home where he had had everything that heart could desire, to his uncle's less flourishing abode. Dr. Dennis was a medical practitioner in a large commercial town in the Midlands, and it was all he could do to make both ends meet, although his practice was an increasing one; indeed, in years gone by, it would have been harder times for the doctor's family but for his well-to-do brother-in-law, who had always been his best friend. Mrs. Dennis was naturally deeply attached to her brother, and she was exceedingly fond of Freddy, who was a bright, intelligent little fellow.

When Dr. Dennis had finished reading Mr. Collins' letter he returned it to his wife, and glanced from her to the children. Rightly interpreting his look, she told them that as they had finished their breakfast they might go, adding that she would join them in the schoolroom by-and-by. Somewhat reluctantly the young folks left the room, and repaired to the apartment which had been formerly their nursery, but, now that they were school-children, was used as a room where they learnt their lessons in the evenings, and could follow their own pursuits without interruption.

"Mother might as well have told us who Uncle Frederick is going to marry," said Claude, in a slightly injured tone.

"Some old frump, I expect," Edwin replied; "I wonder how Freddy will like having a step-mother."

"Poor Freddy!" sighed Poppy, sympathetically, recalling all the stories she had heard of unkind step-mothers; "it will be very hard lines for him, won't it?"

"Oh, I don't know that!" Edwin exclaimed quickly. "So far he has had everything his own way, and he's very selfish. I noticed that when I was at Marldon Court at Easter. He wouldn't let me ride his pony, though uncle asked him if he would and was vexed because he wouldn't; and he'd hardly allow me to touch his pet rabbits; and he got quite nasty when his dog took a fancy to me. All the same he's a jolly little chap," he allowed, "and willing to do you a good turn—that is, if it doesn't put him out of the way to do it."

Claude and Poppy laughed at the conclusion of their brother's sentence, and continued to discuss their cousin till the door at length opened to admit their mother. Immediately they began to ply her with questions; but she held up a silencing hand, saying that if they would listen quietly she would tell them all she knew herself concerning their uncle's approaching marriage.

"He is going to marry a young lady who has been visiting in the neighbourhood of Marldon Court," she commenced to explain, "and he says Freddy likes her, which is extremely satisfactory. There is no reason why the wedding should be delayed, so it is to take place very shortly, and Freddy is to come here whilst his father and step-mother go abroad."

"Is he coming for months, mother?" Edwin asked seriously.

"Yes; very likely he will stay with us till Christmas. Your uncle suggests that he should go to school with you boys, and I am sure that will be the best plan."

"Freddy has never been to school, has he?" questioned Claude.

"No: he has been educated by a governess up to the present."

"And a fine time he led her, judging from his own accounts," said Edwin laughing; "I believe she let him do as he pleased for the sake of a peaceful life."

"I am afraid he is rather a spoilt child," admitted Mrs. Dennis; "but I am sure he is a very affectionate little fellow. Your uncle says he is certain the wife he has chosen will prove a kind step-mother, and if so, he is acting wisely for Freddy's sake. Your father and I will, of course, be invited to the wedding, which will be at the end of the month."

"So soon as that!" exclaimed the children in surprise.

"Yes. It will be a very quiet wedding. The bride—Miss Seymour she is called—is to be married from the Vicarage at Marldon; the Vicar is her uncle, and she has often visited him before this year, so your uncle and Freddy have known her some time. After the wedding your father and I will bring Freddy back with us."

"I suppose they have bride cakes at quiet weddings, don't they?" asked Poppy, anxiously, at which her mother and brothers laughed, and the former replied that she was not certain upon the point.

"I wonder how Freddy will like going to school," Edwin said, reflectively; "he's sure not to like it at first. I shall warn him not to be too important with the boys; he's younger than I am, so I suppose I shall have to stick by him if he gets into trouble, especially as he's our cousin."

"Why should he get into trouble?" Mrs. Dennis inquired. "He always appeared to me very good-tempered."

"Oh, yes!" Edwin agreed; "but, he's inclined to be meddlesome, and to interfere with what doesn't concern him. He has such a good opinion of himself that he thinks what he does and says must be right."

"Then he must be very conceited!" Poppy exclaimed with decision.

"You see, he has had no sister or brother to point out his failings to him," Mrs. Dennis said excusingly. "You must be kind to him, children, for he will be your guest, and I want him to have a happy time whilst he is with us. It will be a great change for him here in many respects. No doubt he will feel the separation from his father, for they have always been so devoted to each other; and he will miss his pony and his numerous pets, but I hope he will be quite compensated for all he loses by your friendship and love. The society of young folks is what he most wants; hitherto, he has lived with grown-up people only."

"It must have been very dull for him sometimes," said Claude; "but of course there are so many more ways of amusing oneself in the country than in the town. I wonder what he will think of this place. It will seem odd to him to live in a house in a street, with no garden."

"And a grocer's shop opposite," added Edwin, who was standing by the window looking out.

"Well, that's very convenient," Poppy said in a matter-of-fact tone. "It is a mile from Marldon Court to the village, and then there's only an all-sorts shop there. Mother, when you lived with Uncle Frederick before you married father, didn't you find it very inconvenient about the shopping?"

"No, my dear, for we used to keep a good stock of everything in the house. Now, I must leave you, and go and write to Uncle Frederick. Have you any messages for him? Shall I send him your congratulations?

"Please, mother," all three answered, and Poppy added: "Say I hope our new auntie will be very nice."

FREDDY ON HIS PONY.

"And what message will you send to Freddy?" Mrs. Dennis asked with a smile.

"Tell him we're glad he likes Miss Seymour," Claude said seriously, "and that we're looking forward to seeing him."

"And that he'd better leave his meddlesome tricks behind him at Marldon Court, for there's no room for them here!" Edwin cried laughingly. "Oh, well, mother, you can leave that out, if you please!" he said, as Mrs. Dennis shook her head; then, as she left the room, he turned to his sister and brother, and remarked with sudden gravity: "I do hope mother won't be disappointed in Freddy, but she really doesn't know what he's like, for he was always on his best behaviour in her presence."

"He's very fond of her," Claude replied, "so perhaps he won't mind obeying her when he comes here to stay."

"I don't believe he ever really obeyed anyone in his life," Edwin said, "but he'll have to begin, and I don't suppose he'll like it. Well, we have had unexpected news to-day. I don't know whether to call it good news or not."

Edwin was a thoughtful, observant boy, and during his fortnight's visit to Marldon Court in the spring he had spent most of the time in his cousin's society, and had formed a fair estimate of his character. Would Freddy expect the members of his uncle's household to give way to him, to study his pleasure, and to bend to his imperious will? If so, he would find out he had made a mistake, for Dr. Dennis— "Uncle Jo," as Freddy called him— exacted strict obedience from his children, and would require it from his little nephew too.

Chapter II
Freddy's Arrival

It was on an evening towards the end of September, that the train by which Freddy Collins and his aunt and uncle had travelled from Devonshire slowed into the railway station of the town of B—, where the Dennis family resided. Freddy, a well-grown boy with a healthy complexion and blue eyes, was feeling very tired and slightly depressed. The previous day had been a long and exciting one, beginning with the marriage of Miss Seymour and Mr. Collins, and the departure of the bridal pair in the morning, and concluding with a tea in the village schoolroom, and an entertainment for the villagers in the evening.

Though Freddy really liked his step-mother, who, as Mrs. Dennis had been delighted to find, was in every way likely to make her brother a good wife, and was very bright and attractive, he did not approve of the plans she and his father had made for a long trip on the Continent, for he did not at all relish the idea of being banished for nearly three months from his home, as would be the case if Mr. and Mrs. Collins did not return till Christmas, though he had often wished to visit his relatives at B—. As the train had sped farther and farther from the wooded county of his birth, which he had never left before, he had grown quieter and quieter, and at last had fallen asleep, never awakening till his uncle touched him on the shoulder, saying: "Wake up, my boy. Here we are at last."

The next minute Freddy was standing on the station platform, being welcomed by his cousins, who had all come to meet him and their parents. They talked so much and so fast that he felt quite bewildered; but finally Edwin and Claude took him between them and marched him off, saying that they would walk home as it was not far to go, and the others would follow as soon as Dr. Dennis had seen to the luggage.

"I expect you're hungry after your long journey," said Edwin kindly, "but there's a jolly tea waiting for you. The wedding went off all right, I suppose? I say, what a good thing it is you like your step-mother!"

"Oh, she's all right," Freddy answered promptly. "I think you'll be sure to like her too. She and father are gone abroad, you know, and they wouldn't let me stay at Marldon Court with the servants."

"You'll be better with us," Claude told his cousin; "you'll like it at school after a while, and we shan't let you be dull. You've grown a good bit since I saw you last, Freddy; you're taller than I am now."

"Yes," Freddy assented, smiling complacently, "I believe I am; and I'm not so old as you by nearly two months. What a dirty place B— seems to be," he proceeded, glancing about him in the gathering dusk, "and how narrow this street is!"

"Yes, this is an old part of the town; in the newer parts the streets are wider," Edwin explained. "This is High Street; most of the business is done here; and here we are at home."

"At home!" Freddy cried, in blank astonishment. "Why, you don't mean to say this is Uncle Jo's house?" he questioned.

"Certainly it is," Edwin answered; "I thought you knew we lived in the main street."

Freddy made no response, but the quick look he cast around him was more eloquent than words. He followed his cousins into the house in silence, and after hanging up his coat in the hall, was led into the dining-room, where a substantial meal was spread invitingly on the table, and a bright welcoming fire burned in the grate, for the evening was chilly, though it was only early autumn. A few minutes later Mrs. Dennis and Poppy arrived. The former explained that her husband had gone to see the doctor who had kindly attended his patients during his brief absence from home; and as soon as she had taken off her hat and cloak they all took their seats at the tea-table.

Freddy's spirits revived during the meal, and he gave his cousins a glowing account of the wedding. Poppy, who had hitherto considered that a step-mother must be a disagreeable person, was astonished to find that this one was young and pretty, and that Freddy heartily admired and liked her, whilst the idea of being jealous of her in any way had never occurred to him.

"Of course he doesn't remember his own mother, that's why he doesn't mind," reasoned the little girl to herself. "Still, I think it is very nice of him not to mind all the same."

"I hope father will soon be home," Edwin remarked presently; "I am sure he must want his tea; but I should not be surprised if he has gone to see old Mr. Henley."

"Is Mr. Henley ill?" Mrs. Dennis inquired.

"WAKE UP, MY BOY. HERE WE ARE AT LAST."

"Yes. He sent for father yesterday; I heard the servant who called say Mr. Henley would be dreadfully put out when he heard father was away, because he likes him better than any other doctor in the town."

There was a ring of loving pride in the boy's voice as he spoke, for he felt great pleasure in the knowledge that his father was so highly esteemed, and his mother smiled understandingly as she met his eyes.

"I am sure if I was ill I should like to have Uncle Jo to doctor me," Freddy said with a smile; "he's so kind and gentle, though he is so big. He's just like a great bear in that old overcoat he wears—I mean the one he travelled in, with the cape."

"Oh yes! he's had it for ages; as long as I can remember!" Poppy cried. "Mother told him the other day it was getting too shabby to wear, and he said he'd get a new one by the winter."

By-and-by Freddy was escorted over the house by his cousins. The two rooms nearest the front door were given up as waiting and consulting rooms for the doctor's patients, and a small room beyond served as a surgery, so that the dining-room was the only apartment on the ground floor in the use of the family, the kitchens being below, and the drawing-room upstairs. Freddy found he was allotted a small room next to the one which the brothers shared. The whole house seemed cramped and shabby in his sight, but he did not say so, and expressed himself satisfied with the arrangements which had been made for his comfort.

When the children reentered the dining-room they found Dr. Dennis there having his tea. As Edwin had guessed, his father had been to visit Mr. Henley, who had been desirous of seeing him immediately on his return.

"What is this?" inquired Poppy curiously, examining a brown paper parcel which had been laid on a chair behind the door. "It's addressed to you, father. Oh, I see, it comes from Dalton, the tailor."

"I suppose it must be my new overcoat," her father replied; "I gave the order and was measured for it last week. You may open the parcel and look at it if you like, Poppy."

The little girl immediately did so, whilst her brothers drew near. It was evident that new clothes were not of frequent importation in the doctor's household.

"Now, father, you must try it on," Poppy said decidedly; "mustn't he, mother?"

"Yes, do, Jo," smiled Mrs. Dennis, as interested as the children.

So to please them all, Dr. Dennis stood up and put on his new overcoat, which met with unanimous approval and admiration.

"I really wanted it, for my old one is very shabby," he remarked; "still, there's a lot of wear left in it, and I shall keep it for night work, unless I fall across some poor creature who really requires such a garment. I left it in the hall, but I'll hang it up behind the surgery door."

"Oh, I don't think you'll wear it again now you have a better one," his wife interposed. "Give it away, then it will be doing good to someone."

"Very well, I will, my dear; but let it remain behind the surgery door till I see a deserving person to present it to. I daresay I shall soon find such a one amongst my poor patients. I've an affection for that old coat; it's been a good servant."

The children laughed. It had amused Freddy to see the keen interest with which they had examined the doctor's new purchase, for it would never have occurred to him to criticise any article of his father's wardrobe, or even to notice it at all; but his cousins had appeared quite excited as they had felt the texture and criticised the fit of the new coat.

Remembering that this was the first occasion on which he had ever been away from his home, Freddy's relatives did all they possibly could to entertain him and render him happy with them, and they were successful in their efforts for the first few days, when the visitor was on his best behaviour. He was grateful to them for their kindness, for the big town with its busy inhabitants, its dingy houses blackened with the smoke from numerous factories, filled the country-bred child with a sense of loneliness which his cousins could not understand. The week after his arrival he accompanied Edwin and Claude to school, where he found the discipline of daily work most irksome, and his troubles began. In a very short while he had made several enemies amongst the little boys of about his own age, over whom he tried to domineer. In vain it was pointed out to him by Edwin and Claude that he must not expect to have his own way, or try to lord it over others; hitherto he had always done as he had pleased, and had been a person of consequence, but now he found himself one amongst many, and discovered to his intense astonishment and chagrin of how little account Master Frederick Collins actually was. The big boys took scarcely any notice of him, or if they did it was only to order him about, or send him on errands which they insisted on his executing, and the younger boys nicknamed him "Greedy Collins," because he objected to lending his possessions, and rarely thought of offering anyone a share of the sweets which he purchased with his pocket-money; it never crossed his mind that many of his school-fellows, and his own cousins, were not so well supplied with money as himself.

Finding Edwin and Claude somewhat unsympathetic, Freddy made Poppy his confidante, and poured into her ears the history of his woes. She listened, and was sorry for him, but being a shrewd little maiden, recognised that the remedy for his troubles lay in his own power.

"You'll get on better with the boys by-and-by if you don't get cross with them, and are more obliging," she told him; "you think too much of yourself, Freddy, and you want everything your own way."

Freddy was taken aback at this very plain speaking, and he exclaimed indignantly, "I suppose you think I am greedy, too!" Then as the little girl made no reply, but looked embarrassed, he continued: "I hate school, and I hate being here in this dull, dirty town! It was unkind of father not to let me remain at home! Oh, I hope he won't stay away till Christmas; I don't know what I shall do if he does! Everything is so horrid! The house is so dingy and shabby, and—" He paused suddenly, struck by the expression of his cousin's face. "I—I beg your pardon," he faltered.

But Poppy was too astonished and hurt to accept his apology. She answered not a word, but marched with great dignity out of the room, leaving him to himself, a prey to remorseful thoughts.

Chapter III
An Impulsive Act

FREDDY had been a resident in his uncle's house for nearly a month, when, on returning from school with Edwin and Claude one afternoon, they met an old gentleman in High Street, who stopped when he caught sight of the three boys, and addressed the eldest in a gruff though not unkindly voice.

"Tell your father I want to see him when he can spare me half an hour," he said. "I find he is not at home now. He need not call till to-morrow, if that will be more convenient for him than this evening, for I don't want him to visit me in his professional capacity—tell him so, and he'll understand. Mind you don't forget my message."

"I will be sure to remember it," Edwin replied as he lifted his cap courteously.

The old gentleman nodded; then, glancing at Freddy, he said:

"That boy is not your brother, is he?"

"No; he is our cousin, who is living with us at present," Edwin explained. "His name is Frederick Collins, and his real home is in Devonshire."

"Ah, yes!" — and without another word the old gentleman went on his way, leaning on a stout stick, for he walked somewhat feebly.

"What an odd old fellow!" cried Freddy, glancing after him with a smile. "Who is he?"

"Mr. Henley, the richest man in B—," Claude answered. "He's one of father's best patients, for he's nearly always more or less ill," he continued ingenuously. "He suffers a great deal from rheumatism, which makes him rather crotchety in his temper; but he's very kind-hearted, nevertheless, and gives away a lot of money to those he knows who really need it. Last Christmas he gave father several pounds to distribute amongst his poor patients. I wonder what he wants to see father for, now."

"He's a very sharp-looking old man," Freddy remarked, recalling the shrewd glance Mr. Henley had cast upon him. "To look at him, I'm sure no one would guess him to be rich, though. Where does he live?"

"In a house a little way out of the town—not a big house. Father says he lives as simply as any working man, and he has no wife or children to spend his money on."

"Why doesn't he spend it on himself, then?" Freddy inquired. "Why, if I were he, I'd do just as I pleased in every way; buy whatever I liked, and always be enjoying myself."

"Wouldn't you do anything for other people?" Edwin asked gravely.

"Oh, yes, of course," Freddy rejoined quickly, looking rather ashamed of his selfish speech.

"You've always plenty of money for all you want," Claude reminded his cousin. "Uncle Frederick gives you such a good allowance of pocket-money; much more than we get."

"Why don't you ask Uncle Jo for more?" Freddy questioned thoughtlessly.

"Because we know he can't afford to give us more," Edwin replied. "You see, he's not so well off as your father. Besides, you're an only child, and there are three of us."

"I never knew till I came to B— that Uncle Jo had so little money," Freddy candidly admitted. "I think being a doctor is very hard work."

"So it is," Edwin agreed; "and it's very sad work too. A lot of father's patients are so very poor, and I know he feels it dreadfully sometimes not being able to give them money when they want food and clothes to keep them warm more than medicine."

"I don't believe anyone is poor like that in the village at home," Freddy said reflectively; "at least, I never heard of anyone. But, if Uncle Jo's patients are so poor, how can they pay him?"

"Very often they don't pay him," Claude answered; "but I don't think father would ever refuse to visit a sick person, even if he was certain he would never get paid."

"I am sure he would not," Freddy responded decidedly; "for no one could be kinder-hearted than Uncle Jo."

Edwin delivered Mr. Henley's message to his father on the first opportunity. Dr. Dennis seemed pleased to hear it; but merely said he would find time to see the old gentleman during the evening, and did not gratify his son's curiosity as to the purport of his visit.

It so happened that the next day, which was a Saturday, Freddy was left to spend the afternoon in the house alone, except for the servants, as Mrs.

Dennis went to a friend's to tea, taking Poppy with her, and Edwin and Claude started off together to watch a football match. Freddy had intended going to see the football match with his cousins, but his uncle had noticed he had a slight cold, and had told him he had better not go; so he settled himself comfortably in an easy-chair by the dining-room window, as soon as he was left to himself, and commenced to read a book which Edwin had recommended to him. But he was no reader, and his eyes continually strayed from the printed page to the pedestrians passing to and fro on the pavement, whilst his thoughts reverted to what Edwin had told him on the preceding afternoon concerning the poverty of many of the doctor's patients.

The little boy had never known or seen anything of poverty at home; but here, in his uncle's house, it was always cropping up and confronting him. The people who came to consult Dr. Dennis of a morning, before he started on his round of visits, were mostly of the poorer classes, Freddy knew, for he had peeped at them sometimes when he had found the door of the waiting-room ajar, and he had been greatly struck by their pale, pinched faces; whilst he had on several occasions heard his uncle speaking to his aunt of various distressing cases in which he was interested. He considered it was very good of Uncle Jo to trouble about other people.

By-and-by Freddy's attention was attracted by a tall, gaunt old man, clad in a shabby suit of clothes, which once had been black but now was green with age, who was trying to sell bootlaces, which he was offering to every one he met. Nobody bought, however; and seeing Freddy at the window, the old man paused and held up a bunch of laces. The little boy shook his head at him, but he did not go away. Freddy had a sixpence and some coppers in his pocket, and fired with a sudden impulse of generosity he rose, and hurrying from the room crossed the hall to the front door, which he opened and beckoned to the old man, who approached with alacrity.

"I don't want any bootlaces, thank you," Freddy said; "but—you look very poor. Are you?"

"It would be hard to find a wretched creature poorer, young gentleman," was the reply in the whining voice of the professional beggar, which Freddy, however, was too inexperienced to recognise.

"I'm very sorry for you, indeed I am," the boy said earnestly, his heart stirred with pity as he regarded the apparently decrepit figure before him; "it's hard lines on you—very. Here's twopence."

"Thank you kindly, sir." The old man grasped the proffered coins greedily, and proceeded: "I suppose you couldn't find an old garment of your father's that you could give me, for it's terribly cold, and I've only these few poor rags to my back?"

"It's my uncle I'm living with at present, not my father," the boy explained; "he's not in; if he was, I'd ask him to give you some better clothes." As the old man lingered, he fingered the sixpenny bit in his pocket, and debated in his mind whether or not he should make him a present of that too; then he suddenly remembered his uncle's old overcoat hanging behind the surgery door, and wished Dr. Dennis was at home, for surely he would not be likely to find anybody who could make better use of his discarded coat. "I say, can't you call again in the evening?" he asked. "I should like my uncle to see you; I feel sure he would give you some clothes."

"I daren't venture out after dark, sir, because I've such a fearful cough. It would be the death of me if I took cold," the man rejoined with a shiver.

Freddy hesitated. Surely his uncle would be willing and glad to give his old overcoat to this poverty-stricken creature! Still, he hardly liked to take the matter into his own hands. Whilst he stood undecided how to act the other commenced to cough, and that settled the question. He fetched the coat from its peg behind the surgery door, and presented it to the old man, who was so profuse in his thanks that the little boy felt quite embarrassed and was glad to shut the door upon him. He went back to the dining-room, but on reaching the window, the old man was not to be seen, having beat a speedy retreat. Freddy wished now he had asked him his name, and where he lived, so that he could give his uncle more information about him; but it never occurred to him that there was a possibility that Dr. Dennis might not be pleased at what he had done.

By-and-by he went upstairs to his own room, and unlocking his writing desk, re-read his father's last letter, and so engrossed was he in its perusal that he did not hear the front door open, and his uncle enter the house. Presently, however, he heard hurried footsteps on the stairs, and one servant talking to the other who was evidently in her bedroom; and this was the conversation which fell upon his ears, shocking him indescribably.

"Cook, cook, have you touched master's old overcoat which he left hanging behind the surgery door?"

"No, certainly not, Jane. You know I never go into the surgery."

"Master says he's certain he left the coat there last night; he remembers wearing it to Mr. Henley's; and now he can't find it. He's in a great state about it, because there was money in a pocket-book in the inside pocket—I don't know how much."

"HE FETCHED THE COAT...AND PRESENTED IT TO THE OLD MAN."

"Well, the coat can't be lost or stolen; it must be in the house somewhere. I'll come and help look for it."

Freddy heard the two servants go downstairs together, but he himself was too frightened to follow them, being paralysed with dismay. What had he done? What would Uncle Jo say when he knew? He ought to tell him at once; but, dared he? He felt he did not dare.

Chapter IV
Freddy keeps Silence

"IT'S the most mysterious affair I ever heard of in my life! Are you quite sure you left the coat in the surgery last night? Might you not have hung it up in the hall? No. Well, who has had an opportunity of getting at it, then?" —and Mrs. Dennis, who had a few minutes previously entered the house with Poppy, looked in bewilderment from her husband to the two servants who had met her in the hall with the news that the former's old overcoat was missing.

"How can I possibly tell?" Dr. Dennis answered a trifle irritably; "all I know is, that I wore the coat to Mr. Henley's last night, and, when I came home, hung it behind the surgery door as I usually do; and—I was very tired, that is the only excuse I have to offer for my carelessness—I went straight upstairs to bed, omitting to take my pocket-book from the breast pocket of the coat. This morning, as you know, I was called out early, and I then wore my new overcoat. The worst of it is," he explained, as he followed his wife into the dining-room, "there were two five-pound notes in that pocket-book, which Mr. Henley gave me last night for a poor patient of mine whose husband has died, leaving her destitute."

"Oh, Jo!" exclaimed Mrs. Dennis distressfully, "supposing the money should be lost? What if your coat has been stolen?"

"Then I must make the money good, my dear. When I first found the coat missing it occurred to me that you might have given it away."

"Oh, no!" Mrs. Dennis glanced around and saw Freddy standing in the doorway, listening to the conversation. The little boy's face looked very pale and startled; but she thought that was only natural under the circumstances. "I don't see how the coat can have been stolen," she proceeded meditatively, "because none of your patients ever enter the surgery, and I am sure the servants are honest."

"Yes," the doctor agreed, "cook and Jane are as much in the dark as we are, of that I am certain." Then, catching sight of Freddy, he said: "Come near the fire, my boy, you look chilled to the bone. What have you been doing all the afternoon? You ought not to have stayed upstairs in the cold."

"I've only been upstairs a little while," Freddy rejoined hastily. "I've been down here most of the time, reading, and—and looking out of the window."

"Then you would certainly have heard if any one had been in the surgery?"

"Oh, yes, Uncle Jo!"

Freddy had come downstairs in a doubtful frame of mind as to whether or not he would be able to pluck up his courage and confess the truth concerning the doctor's coat; but on hearing the amount of money in the pocket-book he had been too frightened to speak out. Afterwards he bitterly regretted having kept silence.

When Edwin and Claude arrived at home they were immediately informed that their father's old overcoat was missing, and joined with the other members of the household in making an exhaustive search from attic to basement, without, of course, any satisfactory result. Freddy wandered aimlessly from room to room with the rest, looking white and miserable, until his aunt sent him back to the dining-room fire. There, by-and-by, Poppy came to hint with the information, given in an awestricken voice, that her father had gone to the police station to tell the police of his loss. This news was an additional cause of alarm to Freddy, who now began to wonder if the police would find the poor bootlace-seller in possession of the overcoat, and charge him with the theft; but even with that thought in his mind he was too great a coward to acknowledge what he had done. He reflected that if he spoke out now, he would be blamed for not having done so at first, so he continued to hold his peace.

"If I told uncle, that would not bring the coat back," he argued with his conscience, which pricked him sorely; "and I don't know the name of the man I gave the coat to, or anything about him. If he is honest he will certainly bring the pocket-book back, and then I shan't mind so much telling uncle, for he will have the money all right."

But the bootlace-seller did not reappear at the doctor's house, and though Freddy kept an anxious look out for him for many days to come, he never caught sight of his tall, gaunt form; and the loss of the coat remained a mystery to all the other members of the household.

One November evening, Mrs. Dennis and the children had drawn their chairs round the sitting-room fire, when Freddy began to talk of Christmas, to which season he was eagerly looking forward, for his father and stepmother proposed being at home by that time.

"I wish you were all going to be at Marldon Court for Christmas," he said, looking affectionately at his aunt and cousins; "what fun we would have! But I suppose Uncle Jo would not be able to leave his practice?"

"No," Mrs. Dennis replied; "and we all like to be together at Christmas time—not that it is ever a very gay season for us, and I expect it will be even quieter than usual this year, for your uncle had to replace those five-pound notes which were lost, or stolen I suppose I should say. He could not tell Mr. Henley they were missing, and he could not keep the poor widow without her money. It has been an unfortunate affair, but one would not mind that so much if it was not still wrapped in mystery. It is unsatisfactory in every way."

Freddy made no response, but his face, which had been very bright as he talked of Christmas, grew overcast. His happiness at the anticipation of the reunion with his father was shadowed by the remembrance of his guilty secret, and he became so wrapped in uneasy thought that he lost a great part of the conversation which followed, until a remark of Claude's brought him out of his reverie with a start.

"I really thought it was father's old overcoat," the boy was saying, "and I'm not quite certain now that it wasn't; however, I lost sight of the fellow in the crowd."

"What is that, Claude? I didn't hear," Freddy said with sudden anxiety.

"I thought I saw a man wearing father's old overcoat yesterday," Claude explained. "There was a case being tried at the police-court as I was passing, and amongst the crowd outside was a young man with an overcoat exactly like—"

"A young man?" Freddy interrupted. "Oh, you must have been mistaken!"

The others looked at him quickly, for he had spoken with great decision. He grew very red, and became covered with confusion as he noticed their astonished glances.

"I mean it couldn't have been uncle's coat," he continued stammeringly; "that is—it's not very likely—"

"I don't know that it's altogether unlikely," Edwin said. "I should not be surprised if the coat turns up some day, and then we shall find out who stole it."

The conversation drifted into another channel after that; but later, when Freddy had gone to his own room for the night, there was a knock at the door, and Edwin entered.

"What do you want?" Freddy asked, yawning as though he was very sleepy, his eyes resting suspiciously on his cousin's face, which looked decidedly perturbed.

"I want to ask you something," was the reply in a low tone. "Freddy, do you know anything about father's old coat? I—I have often thought—from your manner—that you do; and I—I remember that you were at home alone that Saturday afternoon. Oh, Freddy, forgive me if I'm wrong!"

"Do you imagine I stole the coat?" Freddy demanded, inwardly terrified, though he spoke haughtily, with an assumption of indignation.

"No, no," was the hasty response; "but I do imagine you know something about it. If you do, wouldn't it be better and—and straighter of you to own it, and—"

"But I don't! I know nothing about it!"

Freddy lied glibly. He had no intention of revealing his secret, having kept it so long. What good purpose would be gained by his speaking out now?

"Then I beg your pardon," Edwin said, looking distressed. "I was obliged to speak to you; I felt I ought. Of course, if you say you know nothing about the coat I must believe you. Good-night." He refrained from meeting the other's eyes as he spoke.

"Good-night," Freddy answered in a somewhat abashed tone, conscious that, as far as his cousin was concerned, he had lied in vain.

He felt exceedingly miserable, for Edwin had always shown him great consideration, smoothing his path for him at school, helping him with his lessons, and doing him many little, unobtrusive kindnesses. He admired Edwin, and was ambitious to be like him, whilst he realised that he never could he unless he was less selfish; and now the fact that he had told him a direct lie lay heavily upon his conscience. He could not recall ever having uttered a deliberate falsehood before.

"Oh, I am very wicked!" thought Freddy, as he knelt by his bed, after Edwin had left the room, to say his prayers. "How difficult it is to keep a secret; who would have thought that I should be obliged to tell a story? But I couldn't have told Edwin the truth; he would have considered me such a coward to have held my tongue so long. I see now I ought to have confessed that I had given away the coat. Poor Uncle Jo! I am sorry he has had to replace that ten pounds out of his own pocket. Oh, dear me, what mischief I have made! When I go home at Christmas I will tell father everything—that is, I think I will, and I will ask him to give Uncle Jo the money again."

Freddy was not in a fit state of mind to lift his heart in prayer, but his lips mechanically murmured the prayers he was accustomed to repeat every night, and then he got into bed; but it was a long, long time before he slept, for his conscience would not allow him to rest. Never—not even on the night after he had given away his uncle's old coat—had he felt so intensely wretched as he did now, for he seemed to be falling deeper into the mire of deception; he had never meant to be led into telling a lie, and his cheeks burned with shame at the remembrance of how, in reference to the missing coat, he had boldly declared, "I know nothing about it!"

Chapter V
Freddy's Generosity

"I DECLARE the place is beginning to look quite Christmassy already," remarked Claude, as he and his cousin strolled homewards from school one afternoon in the first week of December.

"Yes," Freddy assented; "after all, there's generally something interesting to be seen in a town. How bright the shops are, lit by the electric light! Don't hurry, Claude."

Accordingly, though the air was keen with frost and it was bitterly cold, the two boys lingered, looking into the shop windows, which were certainly wonderfully fascinating. The streets were thronged with pedestrians—well-clad, prosperous people, and many of the poorer classes, who seemed mostly attracted by the contents of the grocers' windows.

"Look!" whispered Freddy to his companion as they were passing a confectioner's. He indicated as he spoke the shabby figure of a little girl, who stood with her face pressed against the window-pane. "Do you think she can be hungry?" he questioned dubiously.

"I daresay she is," Claude replied; "she looks very poor, doesn't she? I wish I had a penny to give her to buy a bun, but I haven't."

"I have. I'll give it to her."

As Freddy spoke, he approached the little girl and touched her gently on the shoulder'. She turned with a start, and demanded in an aggressive voice what he wanted.

"I—I thought perhaps you might be hungry," stammered Freddy, decidedly taken aback by her manner; "are you?"

She regarded him in silence for a minute, then tears welled into her eyes and slowly coursed down her cheeks as she realised that the boy's motive in addressing her was a kindly one, but she brushed them hastily away with the back of her hand, which was covered with chilblains, and answered in a softened tone: "No, I'm not hungry; at least, not very—that's no matter; but I was looking at those sponge cakes; they look so soft, and Bobby—he's my brother—has such a sore throat, and I was wishing he had one; I believe he could eat it."

"Look here! Take this," said Freddy, pressing into her hand, not the penny he had mentioned, but a shilling he had intended spending on himself; "you can get something nice for your brother with that, can't you?"

"How good of you!" she cried, flushing with pleasure. "Oh, thank you, thank you! I will buy some sponge cakes and some grapes—oh, surely Bobby will be able to eat grapes! But he is so dreadfully ill!" and she shook her head doubtfully, whilst her eyes filled with tears again.

"Where do you live?" Claude inquired.

"In Number Five Court, in East Street. Our name is Lambert—there's only father, and Bobby, and me; mother is dead. Father's been in hospital; why we're so poor; and now he's well again the frost has come on, and he can't work."

"Why not?"

"Because masons can't work in frosty weather—father's a mason." She turned to Freddy, and thanked him again for his shilling most gratefully; then she went into the confectioner's shop to make her purchase there, and the boys moved on.

That evening Claude asked his father if he knew anyone called Lambert, a mason, living in Number Five Court, in East Street. Dr. Dennis did not, but he listened with interest as Claude explained about the little girl to whom Freddy had given the shilling.

"It was very kind of Freddy," he said heartily; "I like to hear of spontaneous generosity."

The doctor was reclining in an easy-chair by the dining-room fire enjoying an hour's leisure, whilst Poppy, on a stool at his feet, was looking over her collection of picture postcards, which had greatly increased of late, as her uncle had sent her many from the various places he and his bride had visited during the last two months, and her mother sat by the table, engaged with some needlework. Edwin and Freddy had gone upstairs to the schoolroom to prepare their lessons for the following day; but Claude still lingered talking to his father.

"Freddy is heaps nicer than he used to be," Poppy remarked. "When he first came to us he used to want the best of everything for himself, but now he's always ready to share and share alike."

"Yes, and he gets on much better with the boys at school," said Claude; "he doesn't interfere about matters which don't concern him as he used to.

Really, at first Edwin and I were always making up his quarrels; but now he's quite different."

"How is it he and Edwin are so cool to each other?" Dr. Dennis inquired. "It is very apparent that they are not on cordial terms."

"No, they're not," Claude admitted. "I can't make out why they are not, though. I've asked Edwin, and he wouldn't tell; and I've asked Freddy, and he wouldn't tell either, only looked fit to cry."

"He was crying last night in the schoolroom," Poppy informed them gravely; "he was pretending to learn his lessons, but he was crying, I know he was, though when I asked him what was amiss he wouldn't answer."

The truth of the matter was that Freddy was extremely unhappy and dissatisfied with himself. He could not meet the gaze of Edwin's honest eyes without being overcome with shame and remorse. His conscience, now thoroughly awake, tortured him continually, and he told himself that Edwin would never trust him again, for he was conscious his cousin still suspected him of knowing something concerning the loss of the doctor's coat. Often he longed to tell the truth to Edwin, but he could not pluck up sufficient courage to do so.

Meanwhile, Edwin was very unhappy about his cousin, who, he saw, had a trouble upon his mind; but he felt he could not seek his confidence again, for he was quite convinced that Freddy had told him a lie. Sometimes it occurred to him that Freddy might be shielding someone whom he knew to have stolen the coat; but then, who could that someone be? Certainly not either of the servants, who were both trustworthy young women, and there was no one else in the house it was possible to suspect.

Claude and Freddy, who generally returned from school together, kept a look out for the little girl the latter had befriended as they walked home in the afternoons for the next week or two; but they did not see her, and they had nearly dismissed her from their minds when, after more than a fortnight had elapsed, and they had given up all thoughts of meeting her again, they one afternoon recognised her shabby figure ahead of them, and hurried to overtake her.

"I say, how's your brother?" asked Freddy, as he reached her side.

She stopped immediately, her thin face lighting up with a pleased smile, and rested a big brown paper parcel she was carrying against a shop window, as she replied, "He's better; but he's not able to get up yet. Oh, he does so want to thank you for your kindness to him!" she cried, looking with grateful eyes at Freddy. "I took him some sponge cakes and grapes that day you gave me the shilling, and he could eat them. My! I wish you could have seen how he enjoyed the grapes! Would you—it is not far—would you come to see him just for a few minutes?"

The boys glanced doubtfully at each other, and hesitated, noting which the little girl's countenance fell, and she said in a hurt tone of voice, "Perhaps you're too proud to come? But no, I'm sure it's not that! It's a poor place, I know, but it's very clean, and Bobby would so like to see you."

"Oh, we'll go with you, certainly!" Claude exclaimed, touched by the wistful expression of her face. "You lead the way. What's in your parcel?" he asked curiously.

"It's—it's blankets," she responded, blushing painfully; "we had to pawn them when father was out of work, and Bobby was so ill; we never did such a thing before, but we couldn't starve—it's dreadful to be hungry. Father's just been to fetch the blankets—I told you he's at work again now—and he gave them to me at the corner of the street to carry home, he wouldn't let me go into the pawn-shop. He's gone to get Bobby's medicine."

Neither Claude nor Freddy made any comment, though they both felt very sympathetic. The former wished he had asked his mother to visit the sick boy, he was sure she would have complied with his request, for she was always ready to extend a helping hand to those in distress of any kind; and the latter was horrified at the idea of people being so poor as to be obliged to pawn their bedding in the depth of winter.

When Number Five Court, East Street, was reached, they followed the little girl into her home, and into the presence of Bobby—a boy of about their own age, though he looked older—who was posted up in bed with a shawl pinned around his shoulders. He turned a pair of dark, hollow eyes inquiringly upon his visitors, then glanced at his sister, who ran to him and whispered hurriedly in his ear.

"Oh, I am glad!" he exclaimed, a flush rising to his pale cheeks. "Which of them was it that gave you that shilling, Lizzie?"

The girl indicated Freddy, who came forward and asked the invalid how he was, whilst Claude stood in the background looking on.

"I'm better—much better," was the reply to Freddy's inquiry. "I want to thank you for your kindness—"

"It was nothing," Freddy interposed. He was feeling awkward, for he had never paid a visit to a sick room in his life before. "I didn't want the money. I should only have spent it in sweets if I hadn't given it away. You look very ill still. Are you certain you are better?"

"Oh, yes! The doctor says so—the parish doctor, you know. I caught a bad chill by getting drenched to the skin, and letting my clothes dry on me. I sell papers in the streets in the evenings. Oh, I shall soon be well now!" he declared hopefully.

"I am sure I hope so," Freddy said with genuine sympathy in his voice; "you must keep yourself warm, and—"

He paused suddenly, his attention attracted by the outer covering of the invalid's bed, a large, heavy, man's overcoat, with a big cape. It was with difficulty that Freddy refrained from uttering the cry of mingled astonishment and dismay which rose to his lips as he recognised his Uncle Jo's old coat. The next moment Claude stepped nearer the bed, and his eyes fell upon the familiar garment too.

Chapter VI
Freddy speaks out

"FREDDY, did you notice what was on the bed? But of course you did. I saw that by your face! The idea of our being the ones to find father's old coat, and after such a long time too! I longed to ask the Lamberts how they got it, but that would never have done. We must hurry home and tell father at once!" and Claude quickened his footsteps almost to a run as he spoke.

The two boys were in the main street of the town once more, having cut short their visit to Bobby Lambert after the surprising discovery they had made. Both were greatly excited.

"There's no desperate hurry," Freddy said, in a voice which he could scarcely keep from trembling. "Yes, of course I saw it was uncle's coat; but how could it have got there?"

"Oh, I don't know! Perhaps those people are thieves, and we ought not to have gone to their house; but they seemed very respectable, didn't they?"

"Oh, yes! I don't think they are thieves! The boy looked really ill; and I am sure the little girl seemed very distressed because they had to pawn their blankets."

"Perhaps she was only pretending—father says appearances are often deceitful."

"But there were tears in her eyes; didn't you see them?"

"Yes, I did," Claude admitted. "Anyway, when we have told father we have discovered where his coat is, he will know what to do. Isn't it strange that you and I should be the ones to find it?"

"Very strange. What do you think Uncle Jo will do about it?"

"Tell the police, and—"

"Oh, I hope not!" Freddy interposed in dismay. "I am sure the Lamberts are honest people, I am quite, quite sure!"

"Nonsense!" Claude exclaimed impatiently. "How can you tell that when you know no more about them than I do?"

Arrived at home, the two boys went into the dining-room, but finding no one there, returned to the hall. Claude began shouting, "Mother, mother!" at the top of his voice.

"Hush, Master Claude!" cried Jane, the housemaid, as she came downstairs. "The mistress is in the drawing-room with visitors, and she wishes you and Master Freddy to—"

She stopped abruptly as Freddy, uttering an exclamation of mingled astonishment and joy, rushed past her, having caught the sound of a well-known voice. Claude followed his cousin at a more leisurely pace, and when he entered the drawing-room, found him clinging around the neck of a tall gentleman, whilst a very pretty lady was seated on the sofa between his mother and Poppy.

"Uncle Frederick!" gasped Claude, for the tall gentleman was no other than Mr. Collins, and of course the pretty lady was his wife. "Why, mother, did you know they were coming?"

"No, my dear," Mrs. Dennis answered with a happy laugh. "I have had a most delightful surprise."

By that time Freddy was greeting his step-mother, who explained that she and her husband meant to stay at B— for a short while before returning to Marldon Court for Christmas.

"Are you going to take me home with you?" Freddy inquired eagerly.

"Yes, certainly," Mrs. Collins answered with a smile.

"I am glad," Freddy whispered confidentially. "And yet for some reasons I shall be sorry to go; they've all been very kind to me here, and I like town life better than I did at first. But I am longing to see all my pets again, and it will be nice to be with father—and you."

It was not very long before Edwin returned, followed shortly by his father, and in the general excitement caused by Mr. and Mrs. Collins' presence, Claude forgot for the time all about the doctor's old overcoat. Freddy did not forget it, however, and every minute he was expecting Claude to mention it.

Mr. Collins had engaged rooms for his wife and himself at an hotel, but they readily consented to spend the evening at the doctor's house when they saw how much every one wished them to remain.

The Dennis children were charmed with their new aunt, and Poppy no longer wondered that Freddy liked and admired her.

"Freddy has grown," Mr. Collins remarked, regarding his son with affectionate eyes. "So you like going to school, my boy?"

"Yes, father—now; I hated it at first," was the frank response. "I shall be sorry to leave."

"Perhaps you will not have to leave altogether; I may be able to persuade your aunt to let you live here during term-time, and return to Marldon Court for the holidays. That would be pleasanter for you than going to boarding-school, which is the only alternative, as there is no school for you to attend at Marldon."

"It would be much nicer," Freddy agreed.

Three months previously he would have strongly objected to this plan, and have declared that he saw no reason why he should be sent to school at all, but the society of those of his own age had caused him to alter many of his old opinions. "Perhaps aunt won't have—" he was proceeding, when he paused abruptly, his eyes fixed on Claude, who had drawn the doctor aside and was whispering to him.

"What is the matter?" asked Mr. Collins, noticing the sudden expression of alarm on his son's countenance.

"Nothing," murmured Freddy; "only I wonder what Uncle Jo will do."

"About what?" questioned Mr. Collins in bewilderment.

"About his old overcoat. It was lost, and this afternoon Claude and I found it—that is, we came across it. Oh, uncle!" and as he spoke Freddy left his father's side, and rushed across the room to the doctor, whom he caught by the arm— "you won't send the police to take those poor people to prison, will you? I can't think how they got your overcoat, but I am sure they didn't steal it!"

"They will have to account for it being in their possession," Dr. Dennis said sternly.

He then explained to Mr. Collins about the mysterious disappearance of his old coat, and with it his pocket-book which had contained the two five-pound notes. "And now it appears that Freddy and Claude saw the coat covering the bed of a sick child this afternoon. I shall, of course, inform the police at once," he said in conclusion.

"That is the only thing you can do," Mr. Collins replied, much interested; "but you may depend the five-pound notes have been spent."

"I am sure the Lamberts did not spend them!" Freddy cried in deep distress. It seemed horrible to him that innocent folks should be suspected and perhaps accused of theft. "They are most respectable people, aren't they, Claude? Why don't you speak up for them? And they are so poor. They had to pawn their blankets! Think of that, father; this cold weather, too! Oh, dear father, ask Uncle Jo not to have them sent to prison! I am certain the Lamberts are honest!"

"If they are they will prove themselves so," Mr. Collins remarked gravely; "don't distress yourself unnecessarily."

Freddy looked around in great agitation. He realised that if he continued to hold his tongue there might be trouble in store for the poor family that had had so much to contend against already, and Christmas was coming when everyone ought to be so happy, he thought. What sort of Christmas would he himself have with this guilty secret on his conscience? He felt he could not speak out; but whilst he was in hesitation, he met Edwin's eyes fixed upon him sadly and anxiously, and overcome with the dread of what his continued silence might lead to, and a sense of real remorse, he startled every one in the room by bursting into tears.

"Freddy, my dear boy, what is it?" asked his father, putting his arm tenderly around the little boy's heaving shoulders; "depend upon it your uncle will do nothing that is not right and just."

"Oh, I cannot bear it any longer, I must tell!" sobbed Freddy. "Oh, I don't know what you will all think of me, but—but—I—I gave away Uncle Jo's old overcoat!"

"You gave away my old overcoat!" the doctor exclaimed in utter amazement.

"Yes, Uncle Jo. I—I gave it to a poor old man who—who was selling bootlaces in the street," Freddy confessed in a low, shamed tone; "his clothes were ragged, and it was so—so cold. I went to the door and spoke to him, and gave him twopence—it was that Saturday afternoon I was at home alone—and he begged for some old clothes. I knew you meant to give away your old overcoat, but—you weren't at home, so I couldn't speak to you about it, and—I thought you wouldn't mind-I gave it to him and he went away."

"Why didn't you tell me before?" Dr. Dennis asked reproachfully.

"I meant to tell you, Uncle Jo, indeed I did; but when I heard about your pocket-book with the money in it, I was too frightened, and afterwards I was too big a coward. I know I've behaved very badly. I've felt dreadful about it, and this afternoon when I saw your old coat on Bobby Lambert's bed I was nearly scared to death."

There was a brief silence, during which Freddy ventured to glance at the amazed countenances of his relations; his eyes fell as he met his father's sorrowful gaze, and he hung his head in bitter shame. How disappointed his father must be in him! His tears flowed afresh when Mr. Collins turned to his brother-in-law and said gravely, "I will not attempt to offer any excuse for Freddy's conduct; he has acted with a lack of moral courage and a deceptiveness which grieves and surprises me. After what has occurred, I fear you and my sister will be unwilling to have him beneath your roof another term; however, we will speak of that later on."

"Do you think the old man you gave the overcoat to is the father of the little girl and the little sick boy?" Poppy asked, suddenly addressing her cousin.

"No, he was very old," Freddy answered; "he might be their grandfather though," he added, looking startled as the idea presented itself to his mind.

"I will find out all about the Lamberts to-morrow," the doctor said. "Dry your eyes, Freddy. You must not be a wet blanket to-night."

"Oh, Uncle Jo, can you ever forgive me?" Freddy asked earnestly, immeasurably touched by the kindness of his uncle's look and tone.

"I do forgive you, my boy; but I wish you had trusted me. I should not have blamed you much for having given away my coat, though of course you had no right to meddle with it. Your confession has come upon us all as a great surprise—I wish you had spoken out before your father's return; but I am glad you have had the courage to make it at last. Say no more on the subject now."

At that moment Jane came to the door to say that tea was ready in the dining-room, and they all went downstairs. It was some while before Freddy regained his equanimity; but by-and-by, as the conversation turned upon the various places Mr. and Mrs. Collins had visited during their trip on the Continent, he grew interested, and forgot to wonder what the others were thinking of him and if they would ever trust him again, and gave himself up to the enjoyment of the present hour.

Chapter VII
A Happy Christmas

"WELL, boys; work nearly finished?" questioned Dr. Dennis, the evening subsequent to Mr. and Mrs. Collins' arrival at B—, as he entered the schoolroom where his sons and his nephew were poring over their lesson-books. "Not quite, eh? Well, you'll find me in the surgery when you're ready to hear what I've to tell."

"Oh, if it's about your old overcoat, please tell us now, father!" Claude cried impetuously. "Have you seen the Lamberts?"

"I have had an interview with the father of the family, and a decent, respectable man he appears to be."

"A young man?" asked Claude; "is he clean-shaven, and slight, and dark?"

"Yes. Why?"

"Oh, then he is the one I saw wearing your coat that day outside the police court! What did he say when you asked him how he got it, father?"

"He told me he had purchased it for a few shillings from a second-hand clothes shop in East Street. I went there and saw the proprietor of the shop, who informed me that he bought the coat last October from a stranger—a tall old man, evidently on tramp, who had declared he had had it given to him. I asked the wardrobe dealer if there had been anything in a pocket of the coat, but he said 'No,' that doubtless if there had been the old man had discovered it before he had offered the coat for sale. I think so too."

"Then there is not the remotest chance of your getting your pocket-book again, father," Edwin said, glancing sympathetically at his cousin, whose eyes were downcast and cheeks aflame with a burning, painful blush.

"None whatever. Freddy's protégé must have been a regular professional beggar. I only wish those two five-pound notes had fallen into worthier hands."

"I am glad you are satisfied that the Lamberts are honest people," Claude said, "for I was beginning to be afraid of what we might find out about them, although they seemed perfectly straight. You won't mind our going to see Bobby again now, will you, father?"

"Not in the least. Don't look so downcast, Freddy. What's done cannot be mended, and your father insists on paying me back the money I lost, or, rather, the money you gave away," Dr. Dennis amended, with a slight smile.

"I am glad of that," Freddy replied, looking up with a brightening face. "I hoped he would, but I didn't like to ask him."

After the doctor had left the room the boys turned again to their lessons. By-and-by Claude finished his work for the night and went downstairs, and a few minutes later Edwin closed his books and prepared to follow his brother, but, on reaching the door, he chanced to look back and met Freddy's eyes fixed upon him with a wistful sadness in their glance which touched his kind heart.

"I say, don't worry any more about father's old coat," he said good-naturedly.

"I won't," Freddy answered. "Uncle's forgiven me, and—and I've had it out with father—oh, he feels it dreadfully; and I never shall forget how sorry he looked and all he said!—and we're not going to talk about it any more; but—oh, Edwin, will you ever like me again?"

"Of course I'll like you, Freddy. What nonsense you talk!"

"But you'll never trust me again—you can't. That was a big lie I told you, Edwin!"

"Yes, it was. I knew it at the time, and it made me terribly unhappy—the thought that you could tell an untruth like that."

"I never told such a lie before, and I never will again," Freddy declared earnestly. "It made me miserable, and I couldn't say my prayers or ask to be forgiven."

"But you can now, Freddy?"

Freddy nodded, too overcome for speech. Very sincerely had he repented of the falsehood he had told, whilst the coolness which had sprung up between him and Edwin had been a great trouble to him.

"That's all right then," his cousin said approvingly. "I don't want to preach to you, but there's nothing like being truthful and straight; it's a great thing to be able to rely upon a person's word."

"That's what father says," Freddy rejoined, finding his voice again; "he says if I grow up trustworthy that will please him more than anything. I'm going to try to be that for the future. Are we friends again, Edwin?"

"Certainly," was the cordial answer. "I believe I hear Uncle Frederick's voice downstairs. Make haste and finish your work."

What a relief it was to Freddy to have no secret to conceal, though it humiliated him exceedingly to know that even the servants were aware of how foolishly and secretively he had acted. Everyone treated him with the utmost consideration, and even Mr. Collins, who had been grievously disappointed in his little son, when he saw how truly repentant he was, did all he could to smooth matters for him, and accompanied him to see Bobby Lambert, who was gaining strength every day and hoped to be about again before Christmas.

One Saturday afternoon, a few days before the school which the boys attended broke up for the Christmas holidays, Mr. and Mrs. Collins called for Freddy and his cousins to go shopping with them.

"Do you want all of us?" demanded Poppy excitedly, on being told to put on her hat and jacket.

"Yes," Mrs. Collins assented, laughing, "all of you. We want to buy some Christmas presents, and you know the best shops, don't you?"

"Of course," the little girl agreed, wondering whom the presents were intended for. "This is nice," she said confidentially, ten minutes later, as she walked up High Street beside her new aunt, whilst her uncle followed with the boys; "I like looking at the shops decorated for Christmas, don't you? If you haven't much money to spend you can think what you'd buy if you had. Last year Mr. Henley—he's a patient of father's—sent us a big turkey, and a lot of candied fruits and sweets, and he gave father money to give away—wasn't that kind of him? He's old, and he's generally ill, and—oh, dear me—he's dreadfully grumpy in his manner, but father says he has a very good heart."

"He must be a nice old man," Mrs. Collins remarked, smiling at the little girl's prattle. "Now, you must think of what your father and mother would like best for presents; your uncle and I want you young folks to give us the benefit of your advice, you know your parents' tastes."

What a delightful afternoon that was, spent in wandering from shop to shop. Mr. and Mrs. Collins bought suitable presents for every member of the doctor's household, and so long did it take the children deciding upon the various articles to suit each one's liking that it was past five o'clock before they had completed their purchases.

"The afternoon has been like a beautiful dream," said Poppy happily, as they turned their steps homewards at last. The little girl was carrying a large cardboard box containing a handsomely bound album for picture postcards—her aunt and uncle's present to her—which she declined to have sent. "I think Christmas is the nicest time of the year; I only wish we could all spend it together."

"Never mind, Poppy, you're all to stay at Marldon Court next summer, if all's well, that's settled," Freddy told her; "and I'm coming back again next term—father has arranged that with Uncle Jo."

"Has he? I'm glad," she answered, "for you've turned out much better than we expected, Freddy, although you did give away father's old coat."

"Oh, by the way, have you heard that Mr. Henley is going to pay for sending Bobby Lambert to a convalescent home in the country where he will soon get well, father believes?" Edwin inquired of his uncle. "Yes, indeed, it is so. He is to go soon after Christmas."

"I LIKE LOOKING AT THE SHOPS DECORATED FOR CHRISTMAS, DON'T YOU?"

"I'm very pleased to hear it," Mr. Collins responded heartily. "Freddy must go and see him before he leaves B—, and take him a Christmas-box;

and that good little sister of his who has nursed him so devotedly shall not be forgotten. We will try to give them a happy Christmas if it lies within our power to do so."

"Thank you, oh, thank you!" Freddy exclaimed gratefully, for he regarded the Lamberts in the light of especial friends of his own, and he knew his father was always as good as his word.

A cold, wintry morning, three days later, saw the departure of Mr. and Mrs. Collins and Freddy from B—. The doctor and his sons went to the station to see them off; and as the train steamed out of the platform, Freddy popped his head out of the carriage window, and shouted his last farewell.

"Good-bye, Uncle Jo! Good-bye, boys! Mind you remember your promise and write and tell me how Bobby Lambert gets on, Edwin. Good-bye!"

"How he has altered of late," Edwin remarked reflectively, as he and Claude followed their father out of the station. "I consider he's wonderfully improved. I wonder if he will really come back next term. I expect he'll want to stay at Marldon Court, once he's there again."

But Edwin was wrong, for though Freddy was blissfully content to be at home once more, and spent a very happy Christmas with his father and step-mother, he missed the society of his cousins, and often felt dull without them. He was surprised himself that he was able to contemplate his return to B— with perfect equanimity. It was not that he loved his father less than he had previously done, or that he no longer appreciated the beautiful hills and dales surrounding his home, but that his views of life had widened, and he had found new interests. He enjoyed a ride on his pony across country as much as he ever had; but his three months' sojourn beneath his uncle's roof had changed him greatly for the better. He was no longer always thinking of himself, and planning for his own enjoyment; he was more considerate for others, and, in short, Master Frederick had fallen in his own estimation, and was a much nicer boy on that account.

"Father, I've had a letter from Edwin this morning," Freddy informed Mr. Collins soon after Christmas, "such a long letter, telling me what a happy Christmas they've had. I'm so glad! He says Bobby Lambert's a lot better, and is going to the convalescent home very soon. I'm sure Bobby's a nice boy; I believe those Lamberts are as honest as the day."

"That's saying a good deal, my son. I am pleased, however, that your second protégé is turning out better than your first."

"My first?" Freddy said questioningly; then seeing the twinkle in his father's eye, he laughed. "I know what you mean; you're thinking of that old bootlace seller. Father—" and the boy's tone grew impressive— "when I'm tempted to do anything not quite straight again, do you know what I shall think of, and I know it will prevent my doing it? Why, I shall think of the way I behaved about Uncle Jo's old coat."